Read Anything Good Lately?

By Susan Allen and Jane Lindaman

Illustrated by Vicky Enright

M Millbrook Press / Minneapolis

For my girls . . . JL

To my mom for her constant enthusiasm SA

♥

To my family—Tim, Sean and Nicky, Finny and Jake VE

Text copyright © 2003 by Susan Allen and Jane Lindaman
Illustrations copyright © 2003 by Vicky Enright

Millbrook Press
A division of Lerner Publishing Group
241 First Avenue North
Minneapolis, MN 55401 USA

Website address: www.lernerbooks.com

Library of Congress Cataloging-in-Publication Data

Allen, Susan.
Read anything good lately? / by Susan Allen and Jane Lindaman;
illustrated by Vicky Enright.
p. cm.
Summary: An alphabetical look at some different places and things to
read, from an atlas at the airport to a zodiac at the zoo.
ISBN 0-7613-1889-5 (tr)
1. Books and reading—Juvenile literature. 2. English language—Alphabet—Juvenile
literature. [1. Books and reading. 2. Alphabet.] I. Lindaman, Jane.
II. Enright, Vicky, ill. III. Title.
Z1003 .L59 2003   028'.9—dc21
2002008159

Manufactured in the United States of America
2 3 4 5 6 7 – DP – 10 09 08 07 06 05

Read anything good lately?

an atlas at the airport

a biography in bed

comic books around the campfire

the dictionary at my desk

an encyclopedia in an easy chair

fairy tales by the fireplace

gossip in the grocery line

history in a hammock

information on the Internet

joke books in the Jacuzzi™

the back of the Kellogg's™ box in the kitchen

literature at the library

magazines at the mall

the newspaper in my nightie

orders at Mom's office

poetry on a park bench

quotations in the quiet

recipes in my rocking chair

science fiction on a swing

tall tales in my tree house

updates under an umbrella

a vacation guide in the van

whatever in the waiting room

X rays in the examination room

a yoga book in the yard

the zodiac at the zoo

And what have you read lately?

Here are some other kinds of reading.
Can you think of places where you might read them?
It's OK to be silly!

reference book

textbook

nonfiction.

picture book

romance novel

phone book

mystery

autobiograp

essay

short story

fiction